Be my best boss!

11 management tips from your employees.

by Florian Borgeat

<u>Preface</u>

To all the employees and managers
throughout the world who interact
every day in the hope of making
the world a better place.

To Monica.

A very special thanks to Alissa for
her contribution to this book.

Table of Contents

Introduction

I have been an employee for 25 years in almost 20 companies. Which means that I have had over 60 bosses, since most companies I have worked for had team leaders, service managers, regional managers, etc...

I have experimented on a daily basis with all sorts of management types and witnessed the various effects on the employees, their motivation and their profitability. I have had a few great managers and, unfortunately, a lot of bad ones. In the following chapters I share my views on what any manager could easily do to improve his team's efficiency.

I hope you will appreciate my singular point of view.

Chapter 1

Care

This one comes first. If you only had to remember one tip, it would be this one. This is as easy as it gets: care about your employees.

A lot of managers see their employees as parasites, only there to milk money from the company while producing the least possible amount of work. If you are one of those managers, you might want to reconsider your opinion. While there might be one hopeless, grumpy person in your team, and we'll deal with that one later on, the majority of employees are here for other reasons. It is not for the money. It is because they want to feel good about themselves.

Studies show that one of the main factors of happiness for most human beings is the satisfaction of a task well done, which means, "I count for something." People spend a lot of energy finding out what kind of job they want to do, they study for it, they try hard to find an employer who is willing to give them a chance to demonstrate their talent, they wake up every day to go to your company and spend the majority of their time there. If the sole motivation for all that was to annoy you and milk your company for everything they can, trust me, they would not have made it to your front door.

"I don't know how to care!", "I am scared of that!", "I will lose my influence!" If this is what the voice in your head is screaming right now, don't worry. It means you actually know how to do it, otherwise you would have just asked "how do I do that?".

I know some of you might never have been taught how to care for your employee or you might be afraid to look vulnerable by doing so. Or, you might even be scared to be appreciated in return (yes, some people are scared to be loved). Well, if that is your case, don't worry, this is all safe. And very satisfying and profitable to boot! Because, let's not forget we are here to make money, aren't we? Unless, you might possibly be in it for the same reason as your employees are, which is the satisfaction of doing something relevant. So, as you see, your employee has the same goal as you. It makes your caring task already much easier to understand.

Here are some little things you can do to care:
1.Say "hello" in the morning.
2.Say "happy birthday"
3.Check in from time to time
4.Give some free time
5.Get creative

1. Say "hello" in the morning:

This one is so simple and yet so effective. One of my good friends, an IT engineer, was once an intern for a military defense company. He told me that his big boss would greet him each morning, sometimes inquiring about his week-end or previous night. Because of that, my friend has the best memories of that particular manager.

It doesn't take long. A simple "Hi, how are you?" while passing through the office is enough. Talking about a manager in another department of one of my previous jobs, my colleague once said "I don't really know him but he always says hello, he seems like a nice guy." The day this manager asked my friend for an extra favor, my buddy did it straight away and with a smile.

At the same time, our own department manager would come and go through our office several times a day, without ever acknowledging our presence. We didn't like the guy. And even though we were doing our job as efficiently as we could, our team's motivation sank a bit more every day.

There is a big difference between a team doing its job correctly, according to the task list, and a motivated one that will do the job just as correctly but will also improve on it, bring in new ideas, encourage and... care about the company. Because, if you care about your team, the team will care about you, which means, it will care about the job. This positive energy will bring unsuspected results. It could be that during his spare time, one of your employees might recommend your company to a friend of his or that one of your customers, liking the higher energy level of your team, will bring you even more business.

2. Say "Happy Birthday"

I spent five years working for a big school. Every year on my birthday, the Vice-Director would send me an email wishing me a happy birthday, sometimes with a famous quote or some other kind words. Of course, he did that for each of his 300 employees, but still, it made me feel less anonymous.

On my last year there, the CEO himself walked up to me and shook my hand to wish me a happy birthday. My manager was standing next to us and was surprised that the CEO would greet me that day, as he, himself would never have though to do it. I probably only spoke to that CEO three times during my five years there, but I have a great memory of him because of that.

So easy, isn't it? One might wonder, why does it matter if your employee has a fond memory of you or not? Well, you never know how the future might turn out, who can help you get your next job or prevent you from getting it. Your employee might know your next boss or HE might be interviewing YOU for a job one day...

3. Check in from time to time

Every now and then, go see what your team is doing. Most of you have busy schedules, lots of meetings with other managers or clients, important ideas to think about and you might spend days or weeks without seeing your team.

One of my many jobs was for a pharmaceutical company. A colleague and I were working next door to the Director. My co-worker had just returned to work after three weeks at the hospital for a knee surgery. Three days after his return, our Director came to see me and, after discussing the matter at hand for 15 minutes, finally noticed my colleague sitting at his usual place facing me. Surprised, she said "oh, you're back?"

I had experienced a similar situation myself. I had been on a one-month trip and had been back for a couple of days, when my supervisor came in and, seeing me, said "oh, are you back already? I thought it was next week". It might seem like nothing, but I can tell you that those little stories get shared with other colleagues, and very soon with the whole department and, eventually, with the whole company. In no time at all, you are seen as someone who doesn't care about your team. And, if YOU don't care, why should THEY?

Another reason to check in from time to time, is to see if everything is going OK, if there are any unanswered questions or concerns. Of course, most of you have probably set up monthly meetings where the team is supposed to share everything. But those meetings are usually useless, as we will see in Chapter 9, and addressing the whole group doesn't create the same effect as addressing the individual. I don't suggest that you micro manage the whole company. This shouldn't take you more than 10 to 15 minutes a week. Plus, it would give you an overview of what your employees are doing.

Sometimes, in those improvised encounters, the employee will suggest an improvement that he was just thinking about while doing his current task or he will raise a concern or make a remark regarding some other aspect of the company. Maybe something as random as "I've heard that this is your secretary's birthday and she was pretty upset that you didn't even say hello to her." Or maybe: "I just got off the phone with our main client who is really unhappy with our last delivery". Something that your employee might not share a month later during the scheduled meeting and that you could immediately solve by calling back your customer straight away. Or, by wishing your secretary a happy birthday.

4. Give away some free time

We know you don't like to give away your money. Or, depending on the size of your organization, that you don't have the authorization to give away a bonus every month. But there are the little things that you CAN do that will create a big effect. For example, go to an employee and tell her "Your report was great, the sun is shining, leave at 3pm today". If you do that in the morning, there is a very good chance that she will accomplish the same amount of work by 3pm than she would have by 5pm anyway, with the added bonus that she will feel happy, rewarded and cared for. Maybe the extra time will give her the chance to do something important, like go to a doctor's appointment, for which she would have had to request some time off another day, at a maybe less convenient time for you. At any rate, the extra time bought you a very happy employee and cost you very little.

5. Get Creative

There are lots of other ways to show your team members that you care about each one of them. Don't overdo it, don't force yourself to do something that doesn't feel comfortable, don't spend hours on it. Just a little touch every now and then will do wonders.

Very easy. Very profitable.

Chapter 2

Trust

That one could be a challenge for some of you. Actually, I believe it is a challenge for almost everyone, whatever the position or the relationship. So don't feel bad about it should you not trust your employees, yet. But do try to change that. Or at least to pretend that you do.

Showing people you trust them will make them want to be worthy of your trust. At Bryn Mawr College, a women's college in Pennsylvania, the students take most of their exams at home, in their dorm rooms, alone. It's called the Honor Code, and has been going on for over 150 years, with remarkably few infractions. The school trusts the students to be worthy of their trust, and student after student takes her exams without cheating, feeling honored and special for the privilege.

Like stated earlier, most people want to work in order to perform well, to be satisfied with a task well done. The more responsibilities they have, the more important they will feel. Which will make them even more concerned about their job. This means they will take matters to hand even without you commanding them to. They might act as little managers, without the title or the salary, just because they enjoy the trust you have in them. It is easier to betray someone who doesn't trust you than someone who gives you his total confidence.

There are various ways to show that you trust your employee. It can be as simple as telling him to close the shop tonight because you have to leave early. Maybe even for the whole week! If you are worried he might forget to lock the door, ask him to open for you in the morning. Less risky, and with the same result. Another way to show trust is by telling your employee to come up with ideas on how to improve communication in the department or to let him or her decorate the office or select the brand of the new computers. It can also be as easy as saying "I trust you."

Ideally, you would dispatch this kind of task among all of your employees, in order to have all of them feeling equally committed and part of the company. You will also avoid singling out one person as the "boss pet" which will inevitably create jealousy between colleagues.

The more you can create a trusting relationship, the easier it will be to manage your team and, as always, the more profitable it will be for you. People might start to spend more time at work, bring in new ideas, or new customers. They might also communicate with you more frankly, pointing out some flaws in the department or in the company.

A friend of mine used to always say: "Confidence doesn't exclude control". Especially at the beginning of the process, do check if the task has been done as expected, but make sure it is not seen as a breach in the trust. For instance, if you let the employee open the shop in the morning, call a bit later to ask if he has any questions for you. Or if he was allowed to redecorate the office, ask him to show you how far he is in the process, because you are interested in his work and in his ideas.

By the way, even if you have been with your team for a long while and trust them completely, check on their work every now and then. Sometime, people change, and you don't want to have to lose trust in all of your employees just because one guy let you down. It is a bit like letting your kid go to school by himself but watching him from far away, without letting yourself be seen.

Trusting will also help you to delegate more easily.

Chapter 3

Delegate

Your main job as a manager is to... manage (!). However, most managers I have encountered in my life have mostly acted as employees, dedicating only a small amount of their time to actually manage their team.

Your employees are supposed to do all the work, all the production, the files, the memos, the plannings, the budgets, ... and your job is to coordinate those tasks and make sure that everything is running smoothly. This is the most efficient way to run your business or department. 80 percent of your time should be spent managing your employees. If that seems like a high number, I suspect that you haven't tried it yet. 20 percent of your time is left for meetings, business lunches, important customers, ...

I am actually quite confident that you could run your company by working half a day per week only. Derek Sivers, the founder of CD Baby, the biggest online music store, spent the last six months of his CEO job working only 30 minutes per month, remotely. Nice job. Of course, most of you are not CEO's or company owners which means that, while you might be a manager, you are at the same time still some-body's employee. As such, you might feel obliged to act like an employee, spending a specific amount of time at work no matter whether it is productive or not (we'll talk about it in Chapter 11). To my opinion, if you are simply going through the motions or doing rote clerical work, then your boss is wasting his money on a manager that is not managing. And if he doesn't get that, give him a copy of this book.

Look at a symphonic orchestra. The conductor is conducting. That's it. And that's big! If everything goes well, the audience might even wonder why there is even a conductor with such a brilliant orchestra. But believe me, if the conductor fails, the orchestra will start to sound fragile, uncoordinated, untrained. The conductor is there to prepare them as much as possible, motivate them, inspire them, assess each musician's ability, combine everything together, share his vision and, on the day of the concert, lead them. Should the conductor be conducting while also be playing the piano and a lit bit of violin during the show, then something would in fact be missing, not added.

One of my worst bosses was running three departments with around twenty-five employees. All twenty-five employees were unhappy at work, some were burned out, lots of them were angry and some actively looking for another job. In the midst of this chaos, we learned that our boss had spent a couple of days creating a complicated Excel sheet for another department, as a favor! Well, guess how we reacted when we learned about that! We all shook our heads in disgust and lost what little respect we ever had for the boss.

If everything is running smoothly in your company and you have some free time, then, by all means, do the things you enjoy doing. Create a master piece Excel sheet or a great design, show your team some inspirational ideas. But you can only do that if you are sure that all of your employees are happy to come to work in the morning. If not, you need to take care of them first. Your employees are your wheels, engine, body and all the other parts of your company's car. You are the driver. What would you think if you had a driver who wanted you to admire the final draft of a carefully composed symphony he'd spent hours working on while your meter was running. And then, imagine that he pulls away from the curb with the muffler dragging and the engine light flashing because he had neglected to check the oil?

Chapter 4

Be available

I remember watching an interview with one of the richest Swiss CEOs, a watchmaker, who was explaining his daily schedule. He would wake up at 4 am, handle all the emails from home, eat breakfast and show up to work at around 8.30am. During his whole day at the office, he would be available to his employees, go to some meetings, make a couple phone calls to important customers (note that each time I mention an interaction with a customer, I emphasize important one, for 90% of the cases: delegate). When he went back home at 6pm he would be available to his family, but still reachable by email until 10pm.

This CEO was saying that being available to his employees was the key to his company's success. This is so true. As a manager now, you were probably once an employee yourself, and you might remember a time where you needed your boss' approval to finalize a deal, but the boss was busy on the phone or in a meeting, and the deal got lost. Or, at least, postponed. If you have applied the principles in my previous chapters to your company, by now your employees should be working with lots of energy and creativity. But they might still need your input or permission for some matters. Not being able to access their manager will stop their flow. Their smart ideas or their order confirmation might have to sit on their desks for a full night or for even longer if you are never reachable.

I have also worked for a big cellular network manufacturer. (Remember, I have worked for everyone!) One type of installation was worth $500k.

Once built, the customer had to approve the work and a manager on our side had to validate it, in order to have it billed. The guy in charge of this at the time was so busy doing other things, that at one point he had twenty of these approval forms waiting on his desk. Which means that ten million dollars were sitting there, waiting to be billed because of one manager's poor time management. Meanwhile, the company was trying to find all sorts of solutions for cutting costs. Even worse than the money waiting to be billed was the way all the employees started to look at their manager and lose confidence in him.

This might not seem like such a big deal. But just like a captain at war, you want your soldiers to respect you and feel they are in safe hands. If you have time for your employees, you will look like a king.

Chapter 5

After work activities

I always thought that being friends with my boss was a tricky concept. Because after all, as a boss you have a certain degree of power over your employees, mainly the financially. And every now and then you might have to behave in a not-so-friendly manner with one of them; sometimes you even have to fire people. Having a personal relationship with that person is going to make those situations much harder to handle. This being said, I think that sharing time with your team every now and then in an informal manner can be quite beneficial to the company. Here are some ways to do it:

1. Hang out after work

Going for a drink with your employees has lots of advantages. You might get to see some hidden traits of their personality and also be able to talk to some of them about issues that would otherwise never come up during the working hours. You can also just have fun, which will "humanize" you for some of them. But I would really advise against drinking too much and losing control over the situation. At that point, things could be said that were not meant to be. Confidential information has been revealed quite a few times in pubs around the world!

The trick is to join your team at the pub 30 minutes or so after everyone else has arrived. Buy them a round, stay for a while, even play some darts with them and then, leave early. You never want to be the last man there and getting there 30 minutes after everyone else means they have a head start on the drinks. Keep the mystery. It is good that your employees know you as a casual guy, as someone not so different from them, but you want to keep most of your personal life a secret. They will know a lot about it anyway because more information than you suspect is already travelling from one office desk to another.

2. Team building, no:

I have always disliked the term 'team building'. I find that working eight hours or more per day together should be more than enough to create a team spirit and if this is not happening at work, any kind of extra activity will not help. Also the idea of spending a few days with my colleagues in some remote location always felt like a lot of unpaid extra working hours rather than simple fun. But some employees enjoy it, mainly because they are happy to find any excuse to leave home. If your whole team is really excited to go somewhere together, because they all enjoy each other's company, then obviously you don't need team building. Instead of making a big work day of it, throw in an actual fun day instead of a pretend one that is only promoting some company propaganda.

3. Recreational day: yay!

How about offering a day at the museum or at a theme park? Or just going to see the afternoon show of the current number 1 movie? Why not a sports day, where people can get free lessons in some exotic sport? How about actually all having fun together? No obligations, no secret agendas, no lecturing, no financial numbers or PowerPoint presentations, no falling off a stage into your colleagues waiting arms. Doesn't it sound more appealing to just go and have fun? You might get more bonding from that. Your team will appreciate you for the gift. And if they all appreciate you, they already have something in common.

Chapter 6

Performance evaluation

A lot of companies require you to evaluate your employees. This is another difficult task as some kind of personal preferences will always interfere. Don't try to fight it as it will bias your judgement even more. If there is someone that you appreciate more, just accept it and then pay attention to his accomplishments. Equally, if there is someone you can't stand for personal reasons, recognize it but look at his tasks only.

To have a great team, you will ideally have a mix of personalities. Some more creative, some more administrative, some more doers, some more thinkers, ... and they all come with their package. Some show off more, some are more discreet, some are more impulsive and some more attractive. Nevertheless, you will have to concentrate on their tasks.

You can put some measurement tools in place to help you do this or you can simply trust your own perception. Neither of those two methods is perfect. Figures might not reflect quality for instance. For example, one salesman had only three new customers this month while another had ten. But maybe in five years those three customers will have spent more than the ten together because the first salesman was more careful in choosing his target. Also, someone spending more time on his work might simply be just slower and less organized.

I would suggest that you evaluate your team on a regular basis, by spending time with them (see chapter one), looking at how happy they are to work for you and checking what the customer feedback is (feel free to call a few customers) rather than using a standard HR sheet. Most of the time the yearly evaluation is based around a standard form that does not always work for your team that gets filled out more because "we have to fill out some paperwork" than because we actually expect to learn something from it.

In my opinion, if you need some kind of paperwork to see if your team is doing well or not, it means you are way too disconnected from them.

A word of caution, don't listen to what other colleagues say about each other. Most of the time you won't have any clue about what is really going on in your team world, jealousies, misinterpretation, miscommunication, ... , and a lot of stories will come to your ear that might be false or at least biased. If in doubt, always go talk to the person involved, if possible, in a casual manner.

Most of the time, evaluations are done in order to determine the bonus each employee will get. I have always been against personal bonuses as I believe they reinforce competition within a team rather than unification. Plus, if you need a bonus to encourage your team, it means that the job is not motivating in itself and you might have people that are just in it for the money rather than for the passion of it. Bonuses that are given equally among everyone because of a specific company achievement or just because the numbers were reached are far more beneficial, in my opinion.

Chapter 7

Cancel the useless meetings

Generally speaking, too much time is spent in useless meetings. This refers mainly to group or department meetings, like the traditional weekly or monthly ones (or both). Most companies have a standard weekly meeting. But sometimes, some weeks, you have nothing to say. I have spent hours in weekly meetings that started with "OK, this week, nothing special to say". But nevertheless, it inevitably lasts the full hour, most of it filled with stupid jokes or a one-on-one chat with an audience of 12.

I advocate communication, but communication is only efficient if it is heard. And for this, it has to be relevant. So, do organize a meeting, when something comes up that needs to be communicated to everyone. If you are worried about team cohesion, remember Chapter 5 "After work activities" and let your staff talk among each other when they feel the need to.

As for yourself, you might spend most of your day going from one meeting to another. Most of the time your presence might be required by principle, "just so you know". Don't waste your time "just in case". You have better things to take care of than being a statue in a meeting room. Ask for a meeting report. 90% of the time, a 2-hour meeting can be summarized in a two or three relevant points. Remember the 80-20 rule! This gives you the time to concentrate on the most important meetings, the ones where your decision will matter.

If you are already caught up in the meeting spiral, it might be a little bit scary at first to change that. You might think that you will miss out on something important. Trust me, if it is important, you will know about it soon enough. And remember, you can always delegate someone to be present in lieu of yourself.

To ease yourself into cutting down on meeting time, you could go to all the meetings but announce ahead of time that you will only be there for the last 15 minutes. No matter the length of the meeting, decisions are almost always taken during the last 10 minutes and a review of what has been presented and decided is done during the last 5.

By the way, you could also give a copy of this book to your big boss, mentioning that last chapter!

Chapter 8

Kill the open space

I have to admit I never got the logic behind open spaces. I wonder what brain decided that to have a noisier, busier, more crowded environment would enhance productivity. In order to think, to concentrate and to be creative, humans need a quiet space. And one without too much visual distraction. If some synergy is needed, we have meetings and coffee rooms, or water fountains. Some companies, like Google, even have pool tables. This is all good and sharing is needed. But only for 10 to 20% of the time.

Philip Morris Switzerland was one of the first company to change all their environment to open spaces. After a few years of noisier, busier, more crowded, they spent a lot of money turning their building back into small offices. Everybody is happier now. And more productive.

I understand that building separate rooms costs more money, but nowadays there are lots of ways to organize a large room into small spaces, with lots of fun accessories like plants, curtains, bookshelves, ... If your company is working in an open space environment, do yourself, and your employees, a favour and hire an interior architect to change that. The more privacy and comfort an employee has, the happier and more willing to stay at his working desk he will be.

If you worry that out of your sight he will spend his time doing other things, go back to chapter 2 "Trust". Plus, as an employee, I can tell you that have worked in open spaces and still managed to spend time on private things anyway! Remember, the best way to verify that your employee is working productively is by making sure he is happy to be here, not by Big Brothering him.

Chapter 9

Flexible hours, part time, work from home.

Some people are more efficient in the morning, others in the afternoon or in the evening. We all know that and yet, most workplaces are still operating on a 9 to 5 schedule system. Which means that some of your employees are doing their job at half or so of their energy level. There is a simple solution to this: let your staff work when they feel at their best.

1. Flexible hours:

If you trust your employees enough, and hopefully by now you do, just let them know how many hours per day they should do and let them manage their time. Better yet, let them know how many hours per week they have to achieve. This way if someone is tempted to call in sick on Monday morning because of a partying week-end, he will most probably just show up in the afternoon, work a bit later or compensate during the week. This example applies for all sort of situations, doctors appointments, step-mother pick-up at the airport, ...

Knowing that they can manage their time on a weekly basis, your employees will most certainly be more productive and less distracted by domestic problems during their working time. They will also feel more trusted, more part of the company, happier and therefore, will work harder for you. Remember, it is all about more money for you (!). By the way, if you don't trust them enough, install some punching card machine or magnetic card system or any surveillance trick that you wish, just be aware, it is much easier to cheat with those machines than with trust.

2. Part-time and job sharing

Part-time work is more accepted nowadays than it used to be, and this is a good thing. For all office and computer related jobs, someone working at 80% will produce the same amount of work than someone working at 100%, but will save you 20% on the salary. Obviously, it will not be the case for someone who is building a car in a production-line factory. But even in those companies, there are a lot of benefits for the employer to accept part-time work. For all cases, your staff will be less likely to be sick, will be physically more fit, mentally more awake and, again, happier.

3. Work from home

Most computer related jobs (IT, administration, designers, architects, advertising, ...) can be done at home. The only reason companies still want to have their staff in offices are trust issues and synergy. We have covered the trust enough already. As for synergy,

I personally think it is over-rated and most of what we call synergy could be also referred as small talk and wasted time. But of course there are times where you want to see your team and you want them to interact with each other.

Here are some of the benefits of letting your team work from their home, coffee shop, beach, ...: no commuting, which means more energy for the work, less stress, less risk of running late or having to leave early. And it is way more ecological, which sells well nowadays. It also gets all the benefits of the part-time and flexible hours points.

Based on personal experience and surveys, most people working at home spend more hours on the job than they would if they were at the office, since they might be inclined to spend a couple hours after dinner or after having picked up the kids from school or even at 4am when they can't sleep.

Another significant advantage for your company is that, if managed correctly, you could save a lot of money on office space, equipment and the utility bill. You only need to have sufficient space for meetings and for people that do not want to work from home. I would go as far to say that, in most companies, you could cut down your building expenses by 30%.

Chapter 10

Fire when needed

I wrote this book with the idea that it would benefit employees of all sorts, making them happier at work. Which of course benefits the whole company. So this chapter title might be a bit surprising. But firing is a necessary part of the job, so we're going to have to talk about it. By all means, make sure firing is a last resort; listen to your employees first, warn them that they are in hot water.

But if you really feel that nothing is going to improve, you'll have to do it.

Firing an employee is probably a difficult task for most of you. There is always the blustering "YOU'RE FIRED" kind of manager but luckily he is rare and probably won't last very long as a manager before he gets fired himself. So, for most of you, firing someone is scary. It takes a lot of energy, lots of detachment but it is something you will have to do at one point.

People get tired of their job or unhappy in their private life or want to do something else but are scared to leave. Some have maybe a drug or alcohol problem. There are a number of reasons why someone is not adequate for the job anymore. When this happens, it is very important that you take care of it, as an unhappy employee will make an unhappy team. He might start not to show up for work, which makes the other guys have to compensate for him, or he might be present but complain most of the day, which lowers the team energy. If he is in direct contact with the customers, he might even be rude to them or doing the minimum service, which would reflect quite fast on your sales.

I was working within a team of five IT help-desk guys. We were all quite friendly with each other. Our job was both technical and customer service. One guy in the team was spending most of his time doing personal work. He would give good service to the people he would choose to and close to no service to someone else. Very often we would have to do the job over for one of his unhappy customers. He was polite and quite a nice guy but just not willing to work. Some tasks he would never do. Our team leader never said anything. This was very demotivating to the rest of us that actually were doing our best. It felt like the manager didn't care if we were doing a great job or not. The highlight of our deception came the day we saw that the lazy colleague's evaluation was as good as ours! This lasted for five years. It affected heavily the climate within the team.

This kind of situation needs to be dealt with, no matter how unpleasant it is. Since the guy was quite nice, I guess it made the task harder on our boss. But if you spot someone like this in your team, talk to him. Once, twice, then fire. Basically, the first time you can make him aware of the situation, as everybody needs a chance to realize what they're doing wrong. The second time, be more firm and explain that the next time he will be out. The third time, he is out. If you don't apply what you say, you lose all respect from everyone. It is very similar to handling kids.

In other cases, your employee might show you no respect, especially if you are younger or newer in the company than he is. At the first disrespectful word, show the employee that you are in charge. Usually it will require that you express yourself in an angry tone. It is like a virtual slap. (I don't recommend giving a real one!) You need to be firm and concise. You don't need to explain yourself or justify yourself. You are in charge. And most employee will feel safer knowing you have the guts to show it. (again, just like with kids) I do encourage talking and explaining yourself but that has to be done when the climate is calm. In a case where someone shows a lack of respect towards you, act firmly and leave. The day after you can talk to him in a nicer way.

These kinds of situations will happen and this is why I don't recommend getting too close to your employee, as it will make the task harder. Remember that this is a workplace. I wish nothing more than that all workplaces could be happy places. But every now and then, you will need to show that despite all the good will, you are the captain, the conductor, the boss.

Chapter 11

Praise and raise

My best friend works for a consulting company, travelling the world every day, working long hours, being on her own, talking to CEOs, all that for an average salary. But, she has been promoted three times in three years. So she has gained recognition. Plus, her boss is making sure that the company shows how much they appreciate her work. She is happy and keeps working hard.

At one of my previous workplaces, lots of directors have since been downgraded to lower ranks. For the most part, they have the same salary. But their motivation is gone for good, in addition to one of their former employees who didn't see any possible evolution in the company.

Even though I mentioned at the very beginning of this book that people go to work for personal reasons and hopefully because they enjoy their job, they will know they're on the right track and feel empowered by some kind of recognition and feedback. I spent five years in a place that had no promotional perspective. Most people working there wanted to quit and they were just doing the minimum amount of work, as they could see no reason to excel.

Energy is what runs your company. You want to keep it in motion by giving little incentives from time to time. Those incentives can be monetary, 'raise', or even more rewarding, 'praise'.

Conclusion

I hope you have had fun reading this book and that it gave you some hints on how to improve your team's working conditions, as thereby yours too. Remember, the happier they are, the more effectively they will work. The more effectively they work, the easier your job becomes. And the more profitable your company will be.

Enjoy your job, enjoy your employees.

And... care!

About the Author

Florian Borgeat has been working in Business Administration for over 25 years, in a broad range of fields from banking and education to pharmaceuticals and telecommunications. At the same time, he has pursued a parallel career as a photographer, actor, film producer and musician.